Dark to Light

A Collection of Poems from Doubt to Faith

JULIE CARRICO

PublishAmerica
Baltimore

First printing

Publisher's Note:

At the specific preference of the author, PublishAmerica allowed this work to remain exactly as the author intended, verbatim, without editorial input.

ISBN: 1-4137-7898-4
PUBLISHED BY PUBLISHAMERICA, LLLP
www.publishamerica.com
Baltimore

Printed in the United States of America

To Jimmy, Mom, Dad, Kate, and above all, God.
Thank you.

Table of Contents

Part One: DOUBT

God, I'm Calling

I'm drowning, I'm falling!
The demons are calling!
They're always waiting.
They're always hating.
They try to seduce me
because they want to reduce me
to nothing, to no one.
I long to run
into their arms
forget the alarms
the warnings, the past,
I'm going too fast!
Out of control
out of touch with my soul.
I've changed my behavior.
Now where is my savior?
Are my attempts in vain?
Am I going insane?
Overwhelmed and stressed
I'm put to the test.
I can't last much longer.
The demons are stronger.
God, come quick!
Before I slip!
I'm drowning, I'm falling
God, I'm calling!

Addiction's Grip

As the drugs come quicker
I become sicker.
Host to a parasitic disease,
on my mind and body it feeds.
As clean time gets longer
its pull becomes stronger.
This is backwards, reversed,
strange and perverse.
Urges should be diminished
now that my using is finished!
But I still have this craving
driving me mad, stark and raving.
Addiction will win
if I only give in.
I fight tooth and nail
though weak and frail.
Rationalization and justification,
they only lead to devastation.
I've tried my best
now have nothing left.
I could not win
I could only sin.
I've been defeated.
My strength couldn't beat it.

Grateful to be alive?
No, I only feel deprived.
I must work through this feeling
if I want to keep healing.
I must work through this thought
using the tools I've been taught.
On God I must depend
if it is ever going to end.
I seek Him but He's hiding.
Where are his good tidings?
On the door I have knocked
but it remains closed and locked.
Holy Trinity, three Gods in one...
Where's my Father? The Spirit, Son?
Now the beginnings of resentment
So many God forms yet none are present.
Am I being tested?
A show of faith requested?
Only through You I believe
can my compulsion be relieved!
Show me your mercy
God I'm so thirsty!
Quench my yearning
and stop this burning.

Memories

Old faces come and haunt me.
Old faces come and taunt me.
Memories flood my mind.
Memories of another time.
Cravings are ignited.
Do I want to fight it?
For sinful things I long.
Who cares if they are wrong?
I question what I'm doing.
I'm left confused and brooding.

Struggling with Life

Life is hard so I've grown harder.
Take it in, goes down like water.
What's my choice?
I have no voice!
I do what I must
consumed by lust.
The tension is thick.
Cravings come quick.
I long to fall—
let down my wall.
Wanting nothing
Nothing is something
more than I can ask.
Nothingness doesn't last.
Sweet oblivion, to be numb.
I just cannot run
far enough away
from myself, this day.
All this stress!
This huge mess!
To cut all ties
and say goodbye.
If only it were that easy
returning to being sleazy.
With excitement rushing
this world is crushing;

crippling, depressing,
so now I'm confessing.
Let me be!
Stay away from me!
Let me alone!
Just go back home
from where you came
cause I'm still the same.
I haven't changed —
just rearranged.
I'm missing some pieces
like my forms of releases.
My resolve is slipping.
Something's missing.
Happiness and contentment?
Just anger and resentment.
Why do I fight
to make my life right?
My inspiration is gone.
Well, that didn't take long.

County Jail

Fear runs deep into my soul;
pieces missing, I'm not whole.
Helpless, hopeless, no control…
for me there's nothing that will console.

For my sins I must atone.
Ripped away from family and home.
Empty, broken and so alone,
my wrong doings I must own.

Cells in pods instead of peas
and in those cells there is me!
God, how I long to just be free!
But that is not my reality.

A heavy weight upon my chest;
I can't eat and I can't rest.
I feel cursed instead of blessed.
They're wrong! This can't be for the best!

Deprived of life, deprived of hope;
without using I can't cope!
But I won't go back to dope,
for then a chance I can't even grope.

No life through drugs can there be
but this is no life either for me.
Using and dying or living not free,
or not free and dying to live, you see?

I can't see the end ahead.
I'm full of anger, sorrow, dread.
Give me strength my daily bread
to overcome and hold high my head.

Change

Trying to repair my impairment
in my life of contradictions,
painful wounds refuse to scab
but leave everlasting conflictions.

Searching for intangible truths
but never truly succeeding;
hope is stale but not forgotten
in this cycle that's always repeating.

Half-heartedly changing;
unsure, it seems peculiar.
No resolve always resorts
to that which is familiar.

All the stars are falling
steadily one by one.
The web of constellations
slowly comes undone.

Realizations seem distorted
as foreign possibilities grow.
Temptation haunts me, patterns follow
I'm torn! Which way to go?

Forced into metamorphosis.
Forced to whole-heartedly try.
But does the butterfly rejoice?
Or does she only cry?

I'm Scared

Chills of fear run down my spine
as evil thoughts control my mind
and whisper to me, "It's time, it's time!"
I'm scared.

God or whoever, help me be strong!
Help me not do what I know is wrong.
Give me the patience to wait so long.
I'm scared.

Why must my past be dredged up?
God, I know that I messed up.
Is it too much to ask for some luck?
I'm scared.

Can't we return to the way we were?
Maybe not innocent but almost pure.
For this disease it has no cure.
I'm scared.

All my hope is far away.
All my fears are here to stay.
In my head they play, they play.
I'm scared.

Winter Scene Snowball World

Precious moments shatter.
Rag dolls collide.
Legos lay strewn about the floor
along with broken memories of an innocent childhood.
Gone. Gone forever…
My Halloween mask hits the floor.
It all falls down.
Crashing violently into the unforgiving reality
of bulimia, drugs and self-loathing.
The Real World.
A whirlwind of emotions run rampant
like a tornado mounting fast and furious,
leaving only destruction in its path.
The remnants of a little girl
are scattered in a woman's body.
Roots of shame run deep and feed the disease.
Father hungry?
Trying to grow up too fast
still clinging to my Precious Moments.
Blinded by fury as everything spins out of control
in my winter scene snowball world.
Pinned down by rules, regulations
and my own insecurities.
Released by starvation and substances.
Thoughts are distorted like a tripped out Dr. Suess book.
I think I use people who are really using me.
Using everything I am.
Draining my will, my self respect.

Giving "gifts" as they take my pride.
Hot chocolate would be good to warm up my cold
impression of the world and melt your frigid heart.
I watch the pain calmly bleed out of my flesh.
I taste my own and feel euphoric.
Have you seen my Velcro sanity?
I seem to have misplaced it again
in my winter scene snowball world.
Circles and circles and circles again.
I've forgotten what the hell I was looking for.
Lost along the way.
And the breadcrumb trail disappeared a long time ago.
Predictable unpredictability.
Drama queen.
Inspiration is snuffed out quickly in institutions.
Cousins part, friends ripped away, Precious moments
torn from my hand and heart.
They become invalid.
"Be a good girl and do what you're told."
Superficial smiles all conforming in a straight even line.
I join the herd.
Wake up! Wake up!
Don't you realize I'm living a lie?
Tear down the walls, the pleasantries
that falsify our existence.
I scream at the top of my lungs to feel alive!
Is anyone listening?
I beat my hands against the glass
of my winter scene snowball world.
But everything was going so smoothly
Like glass.
Look me in the eye.

My beautiful green eyes have seen more than my years.
My beautiful green eyes aren't a reflection of you.
Don't be afraid to look.
Battling monsters that live in my head.
I thought they were locked away in the closet long ago.
There may be a few skeletons left after all.
Again my winter scene snowball world is shaken.

Monsters in Me

The monsters take over;
take away my will
take my freedom.
They want to kill.

Lost and desperate,
desperate and confused,
confused and hopeless,
hopeless and used.

Robbing my life,
they won't rest till I'm dead.
Character defects
are their fuel, I've heard said.

I'm battling monsters
that live within me,
I fight to hold them.
They fight to be free.

I've given all of myself
to my addiction,
I've nothing left
for this confliction.

Hope stifles their growth
and keeps them at bay
as I do what is right
living day by day.

The beasts lie dormant
forever waiting,
forever growing,
forever hating.

County Jail II

Like a rat. Trapped. Trapped rat.
Walking, walking, going nowhere.
Trapped rat in a wheel.
Trying to outrun the hopelessness,
the frustration, the loneliness,
all the feelings.
Walking to pass time,
to exhaust the body so a little sleep
can be had.
Round and round and round we go.
Where we stop is....where we started.
Walking to keep sane.
To feel the physical pain, the soreness,
the blisters, because it's better than the
emotional pain.
Walking to freedom?
No. Just walking, walking, walking.....

The Tower

I've been hurt too many times.
I had tried time and time again,
to be beaten and broken down,
so I had given up on men.

I had to protect myself.
I could not take any more.
My heart had been bruised and battered,
my body and mind were sore.

So I began to build a tower,
where I could lock myself away.
Free of pain and anguish,
I worked on it every day.

Hard and high were my walls,
my medium memories,
I built with a hammer of hurt,
sealed with insecurities.

Locked away I stayed,
secure and safe and sound.
Lonely is safer than losing,
but then my tower was found.

The walls that I had built
began to chip away,
as you doted on me with kindness
gently and steadily each day.

I began to change my mind.
Maybe love did exist.
Maybe I had found it.
Maybe you were it.

I put away my hammer.
I let the walls crumble.
The insecurity lingered.
My world was all a tumble.

You nurtured me with patience,
fertilized me with love,
watered me with support,
my gardener sent from above.

I let you lead the way,
to happiness I'd never known.
You touched my soul and heart,
You loved me as your own.

With your love I thrived.
Mine grew and grew and grew.
Until I truly believed
there was love, and it was you.

As time went on I flowered.
My color strong and bright.
My petals opened for you,
oh what a glorious sight!

But I began to wilt,
my color began to fade,
when you turned your back on me,
when I needed you to stay.

When the elements were too harsh,
my gardener left me untended.
My stem snapped and I fell.
I'm not sure if I can be mended.

Has your chest ever brutally hurt
from the pain you felt inside?
Have you ever been abandoned?
So lonely you thought you'd die?

Have you ever believed in someone
only to find that you were wrong?
I was in pieces at my lowest.
I needed you but you had gone.

I'm indescribably hurt.
Oh, why did I leave my tower?
Why did I believe?
Why did I ever flower?

Why did I let myself trust
when history is always repeated?
Once more I am deeply wounded,
again in this battle defeated.

But this time was even worse,
since I was not expecting the pain,
Oh foolish little blossom,
things always stay the same!

Can the damage be repaired?
Can I ever re-bloom and grow?
Do the gardener and I care to try?
Have I the strength? I don't know.

Far From Myself

I long to return
to the way things were,
when life was peaceful
when I was sure.

Things were simple
or so seemed to me,
Can I forgive what I've done?
Can I forget what I've seen?

My kind- hearted innocence
for a long time has been gone.
Ignorance was bliss
but didn't last long.

To myself I am bound
yet torn away.
Efforts turn sour
as my strangers play.

It's been so long
since I've been home.
It's been so long
that I've been alone.

Wherever you go
there you are.
So close to myself
And yet so far.

The World: A Metaphor

The air is thick with meaningless chatter; humorless smiles, false concerns. It drips like honey down the walls of this dilapidated building, sugar coating our true state of being. Sticking to everything and everyone it touches, oozing out of every mouth. It gets stuck in my throat and I gag. Superficial pleasantries circulate through the room. A constant drone that becomes recognized as silence since no one cares to hear anyway. Rising and falling like waves in the ocean that never cease. And I am smack in the middle of it. Clinging to a raft. No stability anywhere in sight. Struggling to keep my head above water. Spitting out the falsehoods that threaten to pull me under and drown me in this sea of indifference. A little salt adds flavor but too much sucks essential fluids from the body leaving it dehydrated. Everything in moderation. Nice theory, right? But actions and patterns show the truth is binging on something. Tearing it apart like vultures, fighting to have sole posession of the tiniest morsel of gossip. Selfishly consuming it mind, body and soul until there is nothing left but bone. Not even a shred of dignity left clinging to the defeated and sorry carcass, innocent or not. Then moving on to the next thing, then the next. Never full, never satisfied, continuing to get sick from the contamination. Breathing the unclean air in turn polluting the mind which blackens the heart. Fed up, I tear off the masks of the masqueraders, the pretenders, only to find more facades, more deceit. The ball goes on oblivious to any form of truth. Dancers keep whirling about the floor around me, spinning faster and faster until I become dizzy and feel like I'm going to get sick. Am I the only one who sees everyone is disguised? I run to become free only to enslave myself to my own lies. Hosting my own masquerade ball which is booked in the same hall with that of each individual. They're all intertwined, our realities of undistinguishable truths and lies, forming one massive chaotic knot which is the world.

My Nightmare

I take steps each day
to fix all that I've broken,
living life the right way
to keep earning good tokens.

I've surrendered the battle
that I might win the war,
giving beyond what I can handle
to gain so much more.

I'm following all the rules,
giving all of my being,
exchanged all coping tools,
modified my whole way of seeing.

I've refined my attitude,
readjusted old behavior.
I've gained gratitude.
I've found my savior.

I'm paying debts
and making amends.
Good goals I have set.
I've found new friends.

But as time grows late,
and I drift off to sleep,
you lie in wait,
there in the deep.

I thought I had left you.
I thought you were gone.
I was sure we were through.
I was terribly wrong.

With each step I take
you are one step behind.
I go consciously forward
but in the dark I rewind.

You haunt my soul
while in bed I lay.
I have no control
in my subconscious you play.

Exhausting my will,
I'm your captive at night.
My head you fill
with tormenting sights.

You test my strength
for the harder I try,
you go the same length.
My efforts you tie.

Are you a stage of recovery?
A part of acceptance?
A path of self-discovery?
Or are you a deception?

Plotting and scheming
to own me once more,
for when I am dreaming
I am still your same whore.

Are you a warning vision
of where I'll return
if I don't make good decisions
based on things I've learned?

Are you an enemy
that needs to be fought?
Or are you a memory
nothing more than a thought?

Am I still holding fast
to what I thought I'd released?
Have I come to terms with my past?
Or am I still riding the beast?

Part Two: FAITH

God Alone is Perfect

My heart is very heavy.
The hurt you've caused is great.
As I sit here weeping,
the hope I had deflates.

The wish I had for us,
it seems it won't come true.
The grief and anguish consume me.
I wish now only that you knew....

But to you it doesn't matter.
To you it's no big deal.
You minimize and downplay,
but this pain I feel is real!

Your words continue to sting.
You've wounded me completely.
I'm bitterly disappointed.
Your actions have cut me deeply.

Still, I pray for you,
even though I suffer.
I ask God to come inside.
I plead He'll help me recover.

I ask for His will to be done,
from this situation to create good.
To help me let go of anger,
to forgive the way I should.

It's difficult to pray
for you through all my tears.
When this burn is still so fresh,
on my soul it smokes and sears.

I love the person you are
but I cannot stand the lies.
As my praying increases,
the sobbing begins to subside.

Through our tribulations
God draws us near.
He answers when we call Him;
all our prayers He hears.

To help us grow closer to Him
God allows us trials.
If we never knew frowns,
we wouldn't recognize a smile.

In God alone have faith!
In God alone believe!
People will let you down.
People will deceive.

In God alone have faith!
In God alone believe!
He will never disappoint you.
He'll love you and never leave.

Road Trip

I've been on a trip.
I turned somewhere wrong.
The road was bumpy
to Hell and beyond.

I've run out of gas.
I've run out of reasons.
I've run out of chances.
I needed something to believe in.

I'll buy your ticket.
Can you get me there faster?
My using career
was quite a disaster!

What's your fee?
I've paid the price.
I've given everything
Now I'll give my life.

Now I'll turn it over.
God, it's you I choose!
With Him as navigator,
I can not lose.

My trip is not over.
It's only beginning.
My course has been altered.
This time to winning.

The road is still bumpy
but the destination is right.
With God as my guide,
my baggage is light.

The Fight

Blow. It blew my mind.
Crack. It cracked my sanity.
Smack. It smacked me in the face.
These things stole my humanity.

On my own I was helpless.
By myself I was doomed.
In that web I was caught,
forever, I assumed.

The spider was closing in.
Oh, that web was sticky.
I couldn't break the cycle.
The enemy is very tricky.

His wicked temptations
vary for each.
But no one is safe
or out of his reach.

Does he lure you with drugs?
Does he bribe you with money?
Does he tantilize you with sex?
Promising sweetness like honey?

His honey is poison!
It is only a trick!
Do not give in to its sweetness,
not even one lick!

His promises are hollow.
They are only an illusion.
They can't bring happiness.
That is just a delusion.

There is only one power
Satan cannot defeat.
The love of Christ.
It cannot be beat.

If you ask Him,
Christ will fight
on your behalf
both day and night.

At Christ's command
the devil must flee.
Then from his power
you will be free.

Satan will return
to attack again and again.
But he will never defeat you,
once you've made Christ your friend.

Life's Storms

When signs of a storm first appear,
you may be alerted to what is near.
Even if preparation was steady,
when the storm hits there's no way to be ready.
It turns the sky from blue to black,
showing no mercy as it attacks.
The violent wind whips through your life
causing anguish, pain and strife.
Chaotic damage is done all around,
shattered pieces that can't be found.
Have faith! Your storm will surely pass.
For as all things in life, nothing lasts.
When the storm's fury comes to an end,
rebuilding begins, lives start to mend.
There's always a reason though not always stated,
when one thing ends something new is created.
After even the most horrific storm,
the sun shines bright and rainbows are born.

Guilty and Blameless

When my troubles are great,
I long to run and hide.
To give up the fight…
to retreat to that place inside.

That place so dark and deep,
that place I know so well,
that place where nothing matters,
that place turns into hell.

The devil's pull is strong.
I never could resist.
I asked myself this question:
"Why do I persist?"

I stand guilty as charged.
The lord knows how I've cried.
I am a hopeless sinner.
The lord knows how I've tried.

Yes, the lord knows everything,
Yet he loves me still!
He knows the plan of my life.
This plan is part of His will.

When I believe I'm beaten,
I'm really not at all.
God's love and mercy are so great
He sent Jesus to take my fall.

I stand guilty and blameless,
The lord knows what's in my heart.
Not by works am I saved.
Faith has given me a new start.

Father Help Me

Even though you're always here,
I still have doubts, I still have fear.
Even though I'm born again,
I still judge my fellow men.
Even though I have been saved,
I still feel self-pity and depraved.
I say that You're what I'm about.
I ask You in but shut You out.
God Almighty, hear my cry!
Open my heart and my eyes!
Open my arms so I embrace
Every one of the human race.
You made us all in your image.
Inconsequential are race and lineage.
God help me become grateful, humble.
Catch me now before I stumble.
Jesus you are so deserving of praise!
Correct me, help me change my ways.
I offer my life that I may live.
Help me to love and to forgive.
Remove all my character defects!
Make praying my very first reflex.
Don't give up on me, I try!

Without You I'll surely die.
Help me make Your will my own.
Watch over me from Your throne.
Guide me, teach me, give me protection.
Grant me understanding of the resurrection.
If I know You, love will follow.
Then life has meaning and isn't hollow.

The Last Resort

I drained all my resources
and every glass.
Taking crash courses,
I crashed very fast.

My car, my sanity,
I've done some time;
more hazardous to humanity
with every line.

To the depths of despair,
to the bottom of my soul,
I found nothing there,
just a big gaping hole.

A hole I filled
with drugs and booze.
Till I ran out of options
and had nothing to lose.

I've given too much
trying to be happy and free;
to get a rush,
to be more than me.

Nothing ever worked.
No matter how hard I tried,
I ended up hurt.
I almost died.

But I got a clue.
With nowhere left to turn
I turned to God
then I started to learn.

I'm dependant on God
to be independent.
I must confess my sins
then make amendments.

Through faith I am saved.
Not by my deeds.
Grace is a gift
I need only receive.

My last resort
was the best decision.
Living for God
I have purpose, I'm driven.

God has forgiven me.
Now I must do the same.
He has lifted my spirits.
He has lifted my blame.

He holds my hand.
I walk in the light,
although it's not easy,
I know that it's right.

Discovering Christ

Here's my confession:
I was the possession
of my sick obsession
for so long.
Living in deception
with a twisted perception
and no discretion.
Morally wrong.

My life was faster,
but also nastier.
I was a natural disaster.
I was falling.
A slave to my master
my soul he was after.
He molded me like plaster.
He was calling.

I found out later
that he was a traitor.
Not my Creator.
He lied to me.
My Creator
He is much greater.
He is my Savoir.
He died for me.

I've tried and tried,
I've lied and lied,
I've cried and cried,
I'm done.
Now I realize
I was sanctified
because He was crucified,
I've won.

No more tears.
No more fears
or wasted years.
They're in the past.
My path is clear.
His voice I hear.
I let him steer.
I'm home at last.

Because I believe
now I receive
God's reprieve
by grace.
Because He loves me
I am set free;
and the only fee
is faith.

In Honor of Kelly

When this poem was written, Kelly was brain damaged and in a coma. The doctors said there was no hope of recovery. However, she has since beat all odds and is no longer comatose. She continues to progress. Thank you to all who prayed (and continue to pray) for her. Praise God for this miracle.

In only a moment
our lives have been changed.
Forever altered
and disarranged.

Our eyes are wells.
Our hearts are weights.
Our limbs are weary.
Our hope deflates.

Can you hear us?
God, are you there?
Can you see our suffering?
Feel our despair?

Father please help us!
We can't stand this grief!
This pain is too much!
Grant us relief!

Your angel has fallen,
but Kelly was saved.
Now she is broken,
and close to the grave.

A talented artist,
a beautiful soul.
She struggled so much
wanting to be whole.

Aren't you the Father
who loves his creations?
You call us your children,
your congregation.

Aren't you the shepherd
who seeks the lost?
Who returns His sheep
no matter the cost?

Aren't you the Lord
who came with the cure?
Healing every ailment?
God, why not her?

She's physically with us,
but where is her mind?
Is her spirit with you
or in her body confined?

Your plan's design
we can't understand.
This horrific event
will you countermand?

You draw us close
through tribulations.
You build character and strength
through lamentations.

Help us to trust you,
to endure this test.
Lend us your strength,
God, you know best.

You are our refuge.
You are our protection.
You are our comfort.
You are our salvation.

You have the power
to restore this calamity.
Answer our prayers.
Birth good from this tragedy.

Moments

A compilation of years
divided into days,
further back turn the gears
on moments you will gaze.

Of moments lives are made.
They are all we have.
Don't allow them to fade
as other moments you add.

The good ones cherish
let go of the bad.
In time we all perish.
In your moments be glad!

Where does time go?
Whereever you put it.
Only you know
how you use it.

Each moment slips away
at the exact same pace.
When the day is drained
they're released into space.

Why do some pass slowly
as others go fast?
We are fighting the flow,
living in future or past.

Our lives are shrinking
as time keeps growing.
Our clocks are ticking,
our moments are going.

Life is propelled
by moments in time,
that can not be held,
neither yours nor mine.

They can't be borrowed,
they can't be bought.
They refuse to be followed
and they can't be caught.

Use your moments with care.
One can't change when it's through.
There's no time to spare.
When they run out so do you.

A Christmas Poem

The greatest gift
in all history,
Was given by God
to you and to me.

The greatest gift
was sent from above.
From God unto us,
given freely with love.

The greatest gift
In the form of a child;
free of sin
pure and mild.

The greatest gift
grew into a man;
spreading the Word
throughout the land.

From the very beginning
his fate was sealed.
But still he taught
and still he healed.

Persecuted.
Hated by some.
When they came for Him
He did not run.

He died for us
upon the cross;
God loves us so much
He allowed this loss.

He died for us
so we could live on.
His spirit is with us
but His flesh is gone.

So celebrate
the greatest gift;
His strength is yours
your spirit He'll lift.

Through Him hope is granted,
through Him we are freed,
He gives courage and peace,
if we just believe.

The greatest gift
was given to us;
to save the world.
His name is Jesus.

If you seek Him
you will be saved.
He'll give you direction,
so give thanks and praise.

You Are

You are like the sun.
You warm me from the inside out.
You are like a mountain.
I stand in awe of you.
You are like the ocean…
breath taking and free willed.
You are like the wind.
You refresh me.
You are like a lion,
courageous and strong.
You are like music,
good for my soul.

The Flower of Love

Love is like a young flower.
At first, it stands small and fragile,
slowly growing from a firm yet soft foundation.
Fresh and new.
It must be nurtured and tended,
soaking up the rays of trust, respect
and loyalty.
Watered by attraction, sharing,
communication and support.
As time passes roots run deeper.
The plant grows fuller, stronger.
From cautiously opening its first petal
to the world, to blooming magnificently, boldly.
Full of beauty.
It has the power to brighten days,
bringing smiles and joy
as it flourishes.
If not tended properly, it can wither and die.
Like a plant gives off oxygen and sustains life, love too
sustains us.
Without it, what is there?
We too would wither and die.

Braving the Storm

The sky is clear
but all take warning:
a storm is near
due as soon as morning.

I laugh at their fear.
I am not scared.
No storm is near.
The sky is fair!

I take no heed,
continue to play.
Tomorrow will be
a glorious day!

So all prepare
for the treachery to come,
they caution, "Beware!"
But they can't ruin my fun.

Windows are boarded.
Flashlights are bought.
Food is hoarded.
I don't give it a thought.

People start to scurry
to safety inside.
They're all in a hurry.
I still don't abide.

To all I shall prove
they're wrong and I'm right.
Can't tell me what to do
I dance into the night.

Without fear or care
as the sun starts to rise,
A drop! I stare!
What a surprise!

The skies open in fury!
The thunder crashes!
I now start to worry.
The lightening crashes!

My world turns black.
I can't see where I'm going.
The rain attacks!
Anxiety growing.

Lost, filled with fear
I can't find my way.
How did I get here?
Now I must pray!

I fall to my knees,
I look to the sky.
I ask God, "Please,
save me this time!"

The lord replies,
"Give up your will,
break worldly ties, and
your heart I will fill…"

"Follow my path.
I'll protect you my child.
Your needs I'll surpass.
It's well worth your while."

With faith so slight
I'm torn, lost, I fear;
I give up the fight,
and the sky starts to clear.

Ever so slow
from black to gray;
my faith starts to grow.
Soon a new day.

The horror is finished.
The damage is great.
My anguish diminished
wiped clean is my slate.

I start to rebuild.
The storm has passed.
With hope I am filled.
Free at last.

Following Christ

Dried now are my tears,
receding are my fears.
My mind is becoming clear.
A new- found hope is near.

When defeated and abused,
I can rebuild however I choose.
I am no longer confused.
To be trapped in myself I refuse.

Hope is instilled in my heart.
From my old self I depart.
A new life I'm about to start.
On an adventure I embark.

Through suffering, God came to me.
I repented with complete honesty.
Through Jesus I was freed.
Now I follow him earnestly.

My life has been reformed,
since to God my allegiance is sworn.
I'm a new person. I've been reborn.
Now complete instead of torn.

A change has taken place,
that my heart and mind embrace.
I have been told by Grace,
there's a new future for me to chase.

To this future I run to fast,
as quickly I run from my past.
Redemption comes at last,
no longer violated when harassed.

From the devil I can not hide.
He tempts me, but him I defy,
For Jesus is who I abide.
Together we fight side by side.

I Climb

Pedaling from the bottom upwards,
I climb.
The path is steep and relentless, exhausting in all aspects,
I climb.
The incline assures a rapid return to the bottom if effort
ceases.
I don't stop.
I climb to the top.
For one brief moment I see everything.
I see it clearly, for myself.
Now I know.
I can start my decent,
coasting not climbing.

Isn't Always

A smile isn't always glad.
Mistakes aren't always bad.
Running away requires no physical move.
It's possible to hunger for more than food.
People you trust aren't always your friends.
Beginnings are born when something ends.
Intelligence doesn't equal smart.
It all depends on what's in your heart.

Rebuilding Life

The first brick of hope is laid.
The mortar applied is faith.
Another brick, more faith,
another brick more faith.
On and on.
Looking up, there is a lot of work ahead.
It almost seems impossible.
Conditions vary causing set backs and
delays.
But the foundation and supports are strong.
With persistence, progress will be made.
It shall be built.
It shall be beautiful.

On Love

Love is acceptance.
Love is forgiving.
Love is repentance.
It is a way of living.

Love is sacrificial.
Love is also grateful.
It is not superficial,
nor is it hateful.

Love is just a word
that describes deep emotion.
To define it is absurd.
It's more vast than an ocean.

One syllable can't capture
this powerful feeling,
this glorious rapture
that sets me reeling.

This Earth is a battlefield.
It can be hard and cold.
But you are my shield.
You make me bold.

You make me able
to handle life's rearranging.
You remain stable
in this world that keeps changing.

You're my driving force
when the day is too long.
You correct my course
when things go wrong.

From this world's cares
you set me free.
You're always there
when I'm in need.

You are my heart
now and forever,
Where you stop I start.
We are bound together.

Can love be priced?
It can't be bought.
It is a gift from Christ.
There is no cost.

God's Love is Sufficient

Loving is trusting.
Vulnerability too.
It's not our decision
when or who.

Nothing on Earth
can make you more glad.
Nothing on Earth
can make you more sad.

Feelings and emotions
just can't be controlled.
When a person is hurting
they don't want to be consoled.

It's hard to forget
the pain of rejection.
It's hard to forgive
the sting of deception.

Through our suffering
God comes to us.
He sets us free
through faith in Jesus.

For every life
God has a plan.
His plots are greater
than those of man.

Turn to God!
He'll hold you close.
He'll give you the things
you need the most.

With every hurt
we come to know
a valuable lesson
and a chance to grow.

Seize the chance
to grow in Christ.
He offers peace...
a brand new life.

His promise is not
an easy life;
free of pain
or free of strife.

If you remain in him
He'll remain in you.
He'll be by your side
the whole way through.

He wants to help you,
to heal your wounds.
For He created you
in your mother's womb.

Let Him in!
He'll secure your recovery!
Finding Him
is your greatest discovery.

This life is temporary.
It will fade away.
As will the trials
of today.

The love of God
is unsurpassed.
It is eternal.
It will always last.

God's Perfect Creations

Dawn breaks o'er the land.
I too have broken.
The sun has yet to show its brilliance.
The land is gray and hazy.
I too am hazy....
shrouded in fog, blinded to all but a few paces ahead.
Incapable of seeing the glory of the land,
what it has to offer.
But I know it's there....somewhere.
I can feel it.
An orange tip appears, accenting the sky with red.
I too am pierced, with the first glimpses of insight.
As more light spills across the Earth, my fog begins to clear.
Things are brought to my attention.
Simple things. Important things. Wonderful things.
Things I had forgotten about since I have been living at
night with all its dark intents....
with all its demons.
Now, half revealed is the sun.
Dewdrops wash the greenery
the trees, the grass, the plants...
all things living.

Dewdrops kiss them all with the breath of freshness.
I too am now part of the living.
Yesterdays are washed away. Cleansed. Fresh.
The sun shows all of itself.
Exposed for what it is in front of all who care to look.
I too am exposed. Not only to others but also to myself.
Seeing in a true clear light where I've come from
where I want to go. Options, choices, realizations.
The sun and I each have paths to follow.
Different paths but they are the same.
Both have directions towards our purposes.
No matter what, each day the sun rises ever so slowly.
I too rise slowly.
Gaining strength, confidence, peace.
Every day discoveries are made.
It is a glorious morning in which possibilities are
countless.
I am like the sun.
Bright, shining, committed, affecting lives.
I have a place in this world.
The sun is one of God's perfect creations.
I too am one of God's perfect creations.

God's Adopted Child

I've been adopted
into God's family.
I will share His glory
for all eternity.

I am God's joy
and I am His pride.
I am His child.
For me He died.

God is my master,
I am Christ's slave.
I have new life,
for I have been saved.

I used to be lost
but now I am found.
My shepherd has brought me
home safe and sound.

His faithful love
forever endures.
By faith I'm forgiven.
By Grace I'm made pure.

I give thanks to God.
He is my creator.
I praise His name,
for He is my Savior.

My Favorite Place

The sound of the ocean
is very sweet,
But it's being near you
that makes me complete.

The feel of the sand
can't compare,
to the feel of your body
being there.

The sea is blue
but your eyes are bluer.
That spray is cool
but you are cooler.

I prefer your hands
to the sun on my shoulder.
You start a fire inside me
that makes my heart smolder.

I'll take you on
the ride of your life,
if you call me your own,
and make me your wife.

I'll make you feel.
I'll show you things.
I'll take you places.
Help you grow wings…

So we can fly
you make my spirit soar!
You drive me wild!
I cry out for more!

I want you with me
both day and night.
Your love is explosive.
It's dynamite!

Adventures and mishaps,
we've traveled far;
but my favorite place
is wherever you are.

The Sweetest Thing

I've waited so long
to feel like this;
emotions so strong
of rapture and bliss.

There's nothing sweeter
than your embrace;
no sight is dearer
than your face.

No thought is more treasured
than that I am yours.
It brings me such pleasure
to be the one you adore.

My dreams materialize.
My hopes come true.
My fantasies are realized,
all in you.

My love is deep,
my love is vast.
It will always keep,
and forever last.

To My Love

We have been up
and we have been down.
The only thing constant
is that I want you around.

I long to be
yours alone;
to share one life,
to build one home.

I long for your hugs.
I long for your kisses.
I long for our wedding,
to become your Mrs.

To say those vows
I am so excited.
Our hearts will become
forever united.

To experience with you
all that life has to offer.
Whether we're rich as kings
or poor as paupers.

I find no value
in material things.
But I'm the wealthiest woman
due to the joy your love brings.

Only you hold
the key to my heart.
I can't wait my dear
for our new life to start.

God's Longing

I am happiest when
I'm close to my Savior.
When I am His friend,
when I have His favor.

He wants only the best
for me and my heart.
He is distressed
when we are apart.

When God is distant
it is I who have strayed.
It's I who am resistant.
It's I who am afraid.

But God is waiting.
He is concerned.
He is anticipating
my return.

Although sometimes I falter,
steadfast is His love.
He is my heavenly Father
watching over me from above.

I long to be
with Him, together.
He longs for it more.
After all, heaven is forever.

God's Plan

My past has been trying.
It has also been tragic.
But I am thankful.
It's opened my eyes to God's magic.

I wouldn't change a thing
about where I've been,
I was brought to salvation
because of my sin.

I'm thankful for pain
and for all of my suffering.
Due to these trials
Christ I'm discovering.

I gave up my will.
I try not to fight.
Each day I gain trust
that God's plan is right.

My faith is exercised
in a program of spiritual fitness.
To daily miracles
I am a witness.

His blessings are more plentiful
than there are grains of sand.
There are no words to express
the joy of holding His hand.

I praise the Lord.
I fall to my knees.
To Him I am grateful.
With me He is pleased.

I love who I am…
who I am becoming.
A life of service to God
is both beautiful and stunning.

Blessing

Thank you my darling
for all that you do.
Thank you my dear
for being you.

Your love sustains me.
It keeps me buoyant.
It is pure pleasure.
It is pure enjoyment.

I love how we laugh.
I love how we play.
You calm my worries.
You brighten my day.

Your love is my joy.
Your love is refreshing.
Finding each other
was truly a blessing.

Let's honor each other.
Not give in to pettiness.
Let's not take for granted
this gift of our happiness.

Let's nurture love's growth.
Let's keep it alive.
So our love remains strong
and continues to thrive.

God's Offer

God offers riches.
He doesn't promise wealth.
God offers strength.
He doesn't promise health.

God offers peace,
although this life is tough.
God offers solace,
even when times are rough.

God offers life,
even after the grave.
God offers us all,
if we choose to be saved.

God offers grace,
although we people sin.
When we accept God's offer,
we will always win.

Fairytale Princess

I am your fairytale princess
in this world of chaos and corruption,
this battle ground of spirit and flesh,
this place of evil and destruction.

From your jig-saw puzzle,
I am your missing part.
The part you need that fits,
the piece that completes your heart.

I am your other half,
I fill that vacant space.
If life really is a ball game,
I am your home base.

I am your dream come true,
I hope you never waken.
I am your right answer,
with me you're not mistaken.

In this imperfect world,
our love remains untainted.
It is like a masterpiece,
that long ago was painted.

I am your fairytale princess.
I hope you always remember:
Fairytales never die.
Indeed, they last forever.

Today

I will not worry
just for today.
To keep from fretting
I will pray.
I will not judge
just for today,
To know I am equal
I will pray.

I will not be angry
just for today.
To be quick to forgive
I will pray.

I will not feel sorrow
just for today.
To help me choose joy
I will pray.

I will not condemn
just for today.
To love my neighbor
I will pray.

I will not be jealous
just for today.
To share others' triumphs
I will pray.

I will not be selfish
just for today.
To know God's will
I will pray.

I will not lie
just for today.
To be completely honest
I will pray.

I will not be afraid
just for today.
For increased faith
I will pray.

I will not be insecure
just for today.
To know my self-worth
I will pray.

I will not be stubborn
just for today.
To give in to God
I will pray.

I will count my blessings
just for today.
For contentment
I will pray.

I will remain grateful
just for today.
For more humility
I will pray.

I will do a good deed
just for today.
To spread God's Word
I will pray.

I will give my all
just for today.
For strength and wisdom
I will pray.

I will thank God
and I will pray,
For all of these things
every today.

It's You

It's You I long for,
Whom I strive to please.
It's You I pray to,
down on my knees.

It's You I follow.
To You I submit.
It's to You my life
and my heart I commit.

This world is tempting.
I try to divert my desire...
from things of this Earth,
to things that are higher.

All of my sins
to You I confess.
It's to You I turn
when I'm in distress.

When my life is hectic,
in You I find peace.
My search is for You,
not some golden fleece.

It's You who listens
when I complain.
You keep my body useful
and my mind sane.

Always upwards
I keep my gaze,
On my lips
are words of praise.

On Your Word
I meditate.
The love You give
I try to reciprocate.

It's You I long for,
whom I strive to please.
This life is rewarding
but not one of ease.

On Judgment

Life is too short
to hold a grudge.
You don't know the story
of the person you judge.

To the one you hold feelings
of condescention;
of what they've been through
you have no comprehension.

Maybe bits of the tale
you have heard or know.
But did you travel their path?
Have you felt their woe?

Do you have the same scars?
Do you carry their load?
Are you in their head?
We are all on the same road.

The road of life
has the same end and start.
The choices we make
are what set us apart.

Maybe that person
has had a bad day.
A bad month or bad year.
Who can say?

Maybe that person
feels inferior,
or has suffered a loss.
Are you their superior?

Have you never been wrong?
Have you never felt pain?
When it really comes down to it
we all are the same.

We all are just human.
We all get into trouble.
Sometimes it's huge
and others it's subtle.

Maybe that person
has not heard the Good News.
You could share it with them
if you so choose.

Yes it sets us apart
the choices we make.
People aren't perfect.
Why not give them a break!

The one true judge
is God above.
For all of His people
He feels compassion and love.

All your hard ways
try to bend.
Instead of judging that person,
make them your friend.

Countless Blessings

Friendship is a treasure
that's worth you can't measure.
Smiling is a gift
that gives people a lift.
The music of laughter
sounds sweet long after.
Good memories can't fade;
in the mind they're replayed.
Family can't change
even if some members are strange.
The miracle of birth
brings great joy and mirth.
Pain doesn't last,
after a while, it's past.
All wounds heal.
We have the ability to feel.
Hopes, dreams and goals
live in our souls.
In beautiful colors and sights
our eyes take delight.
The wonder of touch...
it means so much!
Enchanting sounds
in our ears can be found.
The pleasure of taste
is not something to waste.
We were definitely meant
to enjoy the sweetness of scent.

The passion we feel
that keeps us real;
our talents and skill
determination and will.
Our minds are great
the way we contemplate.
Our bodies are art.
Deep are our hearts.
This world we live in
to us was given,
to enjoy and use,
but not to abuse.
Let's rejoice
and use our voice!
To give thanks to our Maker
our awesome Creator
for our blessings so vast
and His love so steadfast.

I Will

I will jump on the bed.
I will dance in the street.
I will play to have fun,
not to compete!

I will use the good plates.
In the house I'll wear shoes.
I'll sing very loud,
except, not the blues!

I will walk in the rain.
I will have dessert.
With my husband
I will still flirt!

I'll stay up past bedtime.
New things I'll try.
I'll jump out of a plane
that's way up in the sky!

I will wear red lipstick.
I will wear my best dress.
When milk spills I won't cry,
just clean up the mess!

I will throw pillows.
I will own pets.
I will spend money.
Be less concerned with debts!

I will give smiles freely.
I will laugh a lot.
I will hold nothing back
from the families I've got!

I'll lend a helping hand
to those in need.
I will always make time
for those close to me!

I'll be affectionate.
I will dare to think large.
I will greet strangers.
I will sail on a barge!

I will be impulsive.
I will do something rash.
I won't worry about my appearance,
even colors that clash!

I will eat on the sofa.
With my kids I'll build forts.
I will travel the world,
and visit resorts!

I will climb a mountain.
I will swim in the ocean.
I will make myself heard.
I will cause a commotion!

I will believe in miracles,
and magic too.
I will like myself
through and through!

On a roller coaster,
I won't use my hands.
I'll let go and I'll scream
as loud as I can!

For all that it's worth,
this life I will ride.
With enthusiasm and joy,
thanksgiving and pride!

Dark to Light

I lived in the dark
with its terrors so long,
destroying myself
doing nothing but wrong.

I feared the dark
but could find no way out.
In my waking nightmare,
I stumbled about.

I struggled so hard
in desperation.
Bringing myself
only desecration.

I kept growing more weary.
I kept growing sicker.
The surrounding fog
kept growing thicker.

My reality was dim.
My future bleaker.
The darkness suffocating,
making me weaker.

Then a ray of light
pierced my obscurity.
A light of hope,
a ray of purity!

I reached for this light
and I found God's hand.
I felt His love.
I heard His command.

I followed the light.
The darkness it banished.
My strength increased.
All my fears vanished!

I now know God.
I now know peace.
I now know freedom.
From the dark I'm released!

I now know joy.
My reality is light.
My world has grown.
My future is bright.

Too many to count
are the blessings I'm given.
Instead of dying,
I'm enjoying living.

I remain grateful.
I remain humble.
I have God to help me
whenever I stumble.

Where once was nothing,
hope and love thrive.
Futility is replaced
with purpose and drive.

The absence of light
is all the dark is.
God is light,
and I am His.

Printed in the United States
30194LVS00003B/12